Lord,
Let Them
Know I Care

Prayers for People
Where They Are

Lord,
Let Them
Know I Care

William H. Fields

WORD BOOKS
PUBLISHER
WACO, TEXAS

LORD, LET THEM KNOW I CARE

ISBN 0–8499–2854–0
Library of Congress catalog card number: 78–65811
Printed in the United States of America

This book is dedicated with love
to
two girls and one boy
who have enriched my life
beyond measure

Contents

Foreword

This book came into being through the intercessory efforts of a minister for his people. Through eighteen years of serving as the shepherd of a congregation, I came to learn not only the delights of sharing in individual joys but also the burdens of sharing in individual sorrows. Walking the pilgrim's pathway with fellow pilgrims from all stations of life has added immeasurably to the meaning of my faith. Through being allowed to enter the inmost precincts of the human spirit, where facade gives way to realism and where people are their most genuine selves, I have been made aware of my own inadequacies, shortcomings, and failures. In such moments of encounter with things as they are, where no frills hide ugly features, I have been both frightened and inspired.

Many of the prayers found in this little volume are the result of facing things as they are, realizing the insufficiency of my abilities to cope with them, and in utter sincerity going with them to the only true source of ultimate help and understanding. They are not intended to be substitutes for personal struggle, which always results in expanded understanding of God's part in our pilgrimage. They are simply examples of one man's effort to carry on an intercessory conversation with the Loving Father in behalf of struggling members of the human family, many of whom have grown faint in the midst of the strife.

These prayers were first written in a daily diary. They came out of personal eventide meditations when I spend time at the close of each day reflecting on the events and encounters of the preceding hours. Usually, one outstanding impression of the day becomes the focal point of the prayer. It may be some inspiring insight, some great personal need, some mighty question or some profound truth. These prayers were never intended for public consumption but at the urging of highly respected friends, knowledgeable of human needs, they have been taken from the diary and offered for publication.

It is the sincere hope and prayer of this journeyman preacher that these prayers will encourage, inspire and lead you, the reader, to a more profound encounter with God through prayers.

Many people have assisted with the preparation of the manuscript for publication. Mrs. Phoebe Maynard, my secretary, along with Mrs. Sue Muse, a good friend and competent typist, spent long hours typing and retyping the many pages. Mrs. Gayner Williams gave able assistance in reading and correcting the manuscript. For their excellent help and untiring efforts, I am indeed grateful. Especially am I grateful to those who have allowed me the opportunity of sharing in their spiritual experiences and interceding for them with our heavenly Father.

Just A "Thank You" Prayer

Thank You, Lord, for deep blue skies,
For dew kissed meadows,
For the fragrance of fresh turned earth,
For the brilliant colors of autumn leaves.

Thank You for gentle morning breezes,
For grazing cattle on the hillside,
For gangling, newborn calves,
For a young boy's many questions.

Thank You for fragrant fall flowers
Hidden in soft brown grass,
For deep clear pools in gurgling streams,
For soaring birds exploring unlimited space.

Thank You, Lord, for gentle friends,
For practical ideas from knowledgeable people,
For uplift of merry laughter,
For a handclasp of assurance.

Thank You for the faithfulness of life,
For the provision of earth for all our needs,
For energy to appropriate your gifts in practical use.

Thank You, Lord, for a good day in the open air,
For a place to exert physical energy,
For skills to accomplish a task,
For the joy of being abroad in Your world for a short time.

And thank You for letting us come to the twilight hours
Tired, but happy,
Filled with a sense of accomplishment
And able to point to a completed project that can be seen.
As the soft shades of night are drawn
Across this little window of a day,
Thank You, Lord, for having let us live in it
To experience all its wonders.

Sudden Illness

*H*ow can we explain it, Lord? Walking strongly through life, with all the promise of achievement before us, we are suddenly struck with crippling disease. That happened to a fine lady recently. She is a lady of great faith. Hearing the frightening news that disease is running rampant in her body, she turned, as always, to the chamber of prayer. I don't know what words she used in her conversation with You. But knowing her, I am sure that she did not leave her place before You until she had found peace. That's how she's handled many crises, Lord. Now she faces the most severe crisis of her life. At the moment she seems strong. She says she has dealt with fear and found courage, faced pain and accepted its presence, looked death in the face and found nothing to dismay.

But, Lord, there is still the long road of uncertainty and hard experiences for her to travel. All along the way she will need strength to sustain her soul, encouragement to fortify her spirit, and understanding to enable her to be made whole.

Use those who care about her in ways through which they

can serve her. And where human abilities and energies fail, let Your sustaining Spirit complete Your mighty work in her.

We can't understand it, Lord, how and why crippling disease swoops upon us. But our faith teaches that You are not defeated by it. In the knowledge of that faith and Your love, we relinquish even this "hard" circumstance to You. We are waiting, Lord, for You to use it for Your glory in us.

Picture the Child

*H*e's a picture, Lord. Decked out in his untied sneakers, ragged jeans, lettered T-shirt, and prized baseball cap, he is the picture of boyhood. Interested in everything, learning about a few things, his inquisitive mind plunges into the fascinating world through which he walks. Because he is so alive to life, he makes others alive also. Nurtured in an unselfish atmosphere, he delights in sharing and giving. Always on his small face there is a ready smile. Sometimes it is deceiving as it covers some mischievous act and asks for pardon, for beneath the smile is a quiver of fear that he will have to face some promised punishment. Basically, Lord, he wants to do what is right and is soon sorry when he has done wrong.

Yet, as I watch him grow through these carefree boy-years, as I see him take unto himself more and more knowledge, as I watch him live openly and freely, I fear for him. For the passing of the years will tarnish much that today glitters so brightly along his pathway. Time will erode some of the boy-heart trust. In the wake of passing days, will be a lot of debris which has washed against his life and soul. And he will change. One day the carefree boy will meet me as a grown man. One day the swift hug will be replaced by a mere handshake. One day the tender good-night kiss of a little boy will be put aside. I know that, Lord. Perhaps what I fear most is my loss, which his maturity will bring. Yet, as he abides in my love and care, as he lives in my home, may he be given wise direction and increase in wisdom of God and man, thus growing to maturity as an asset to Your world, not a liability.

Please, Lord, give me the necessary attributes to be a worthy father to a little boy who so soon will be a man.

The Common Things

We just take the "common" things for granted, Lord. A flower blooms profusely against the summer sky, permeating the air with its rich perfume; and we scarcely notice it in passing.

A songbird turns its head to the heavens and warbles a melody of perfect notes, and we seldom pause to listen.

A gentle breeze caresses a fevered brow on a summer's day, and we move on, almost without notice.

We just seem to be too occupied with the "big" things to care. Maybe we have just become immune to your constant blessings of beauty and song and the gentle, loving caress of heavenly origin. Maybe, Lord, You're too good to us. And Your delicate gifts, not made with human hands, are not valued highly with us in this age of intriguing gadgets, novel things, and multiplied technical bounty.

Re-create in us a sensitivity for the "common" things. Open our eyes to the immense treasure You have provided without price for our enjoyment. Sharpen our sense of values that we may appreciate the wonder of Your handwork and the expression of Your concern for our enjoyment in the house of this world where You are, Father.

We just take them for granted, Lord—the "common" things of our existence. But when we pause and ponder, we discover that all You give is amazingly uncommon and wonderfully made.

Solitude and Resolution

*H*e just sat there rocking in the cool morning shade, Lord.
For sixty-five years, his life's companion had been with him.
But this morning her earthly journey was ended, and she
passed on to new adventures and opportunities. He heard
the word of her death. There was no hysterical explosion on
his part, no loud wailing, no resounding lament—just quiet,
dignified, trusting acceptance. Kindly he spoke of her death.
"She isn't suffering now. She wasn't afraid, and death is a
grand part of life." Having said his piece he sat silently
rocking, no longer a part of the confused world of final prep-
arations. He escaped into the world of fond memories, long
ago days when in the vigor of youth he had pledged his faith
and love to the maiden of his choice. In a distant voice, he
recalled the tender moments when children came into their
care, trying moments when minds and dreams clashed,
hurtful moments when hopes were lost, sorrowful moments
when bereavement entered the door of their lives, joyous
moments when achievements came after long struggle,
reflective moments when together they stood looking back
across the years and all that made them meaningful, thankful

moments when blessings sprang up like beautiful flowers and garlanded their lives.

Now he must continue the journey alone, Father. He isn't afraid. He knows that he, too, will soon round the final bend in the road and pass to the other side of the hill. He will be lonely. He will be sad. But, Father, he will add to all our lives a dimension which we so desperately need, the dimension of serenity, serenity which has its roots in trust and abiding faith. Give us the grace to learn from this faithful, ancient soul. And increase his faith as he journeys on.

He's just sitting, rocking, remembering, and being strengthened, Father. And from his strength we all draw courage and faith.

The Graduates

They're so young looking, Lord. Seeing them, we want to just put our arm about their shoulders and guide them along some high avenue of worth. Yet, the time for that is mostly past. The crossroads has been achieved, and now each must choose the way he will go. Remembering our own feelings when the security of home was left behind, we feel for them. We are anxious, Father. We want what is good and right for them. But no longer can we make their choices. They're grown up. They're graduating—commencing life—and must now struggle to be adults in an adult world.

We're thankful for their achievements, their expressed ability, their interests and their growth.

We're thankful also for their coming opportunities, the challenges, the struggles, the successes, the failures—all that compose the package of life.

Give them wisdom, courage, high ambitions, strong character, and deep faith. They will need these, Lord.

They're so young, so unprotected, so vulnerable. But they're Yours, Lord, and to Your care we entrust them even more than ever before.

The Broken Heart

*H*ow do you mend a broken heart, Lord? Is there some formula, some scheme, some method upon which we can rely to restructure a soul that has sustained a massive fracture?

Is it possible to soften the burden of another's guilt when it strikes so cruelly at the ones we love?

Long searching has revealed no way out of the dark corner of disappointment which is being suffered by some of Your choice children. All the cliches have been uttered, muttered, and stuttered. But, Lord, the hurt of broken hearts still abides. It immobilizes some, frightens others, deranges a few, and burdens all.

Give us some light to follow as we go through these trying times. We do not ask to be released from our obligations to face life as it comes; we do ask for light that we may walk safely through the unknown. Maybe that is all we need—light and a little time—for the healing of the broken hearts.

The Nostalgic Review

They blend together, Lord—these passing years. Looking back, we can see but a dream that is past. From those bygone periods we draw inspiration, gain some insight and dispel some fears. Mistakes stand out clearly from this vantage point of the present; and, had we the ability, we would call them back to correct them. But, Lord, they are done and gone. Our lives have been directed to some degree by them. There is no return path, though we long for it at times with yearning hearts. So we can only place the past into the vault of Your care, asking that You forgive our "wrongs" and magnify our "rights." For there is much that is right carved into the timber of the passing years. Perhaps it is so common with most of us that we take it for granted and magnify the exceptional—the wrong—out of proportion. Give us perspective, Lord, as we measure our lives today against the yardstick of the years. Let not one view become dominant, but with Your eternal wisdom may we see the picture clearly and wholely.

Then Lord, give us courage to face the tomorrows of life. They're like a frightening blank space for which we have no answer. Our wisdom has been mercifully limited by Your wisdom. Could we see clearly through the mist of tomorrow, we would not know the wonder of surprise's joy—the joy of unexpected discovery—or the majesty of growth through adjustment.

Yet, Lord, we want the answer to the equation of the future before the problem of tomorrow is available to be solved. Teach us the thrill of living by faith as You give faith to us. Teach us the glory of trust as You direct us through the maze of the unknown.

Teach us the value of patience as we weave the strands of tomorrow into the fabric of life.

Then we shall stand in every present and look back in peace even as we look forward in hope. Then, Lord, will the years blend together in purpose through hope, by faith; and we shall know indeed the meaning of life.

The Lonely Sojourner

She's a constant chatterbox, Lord. Hyperactive and keen of mind, she doesn't wear well. Some folks turn her off quickly. Others sit bored while she goes on and on. Yet, Lord, she's a lonely person. She's a stranger in the land. She wants so much to belong. Behind that nervous laugh and constant chatter is a person crying out for love and friendship and peace.

I can hear her, Lord, but I don't know how to answer. There are no simple cures for heartache and loneliness. Being real is so frightening for others to accept. That is why we build walls of frivolity around ourselves. That's the way we cover up our hurts and despairs. But You know us, Lord. You know her better than she knows herself. Somehow let her see how much You care, how much You love. And help those of us who have to endure her chatter to grasp the opportunities to support her as they arise.

She's afraid and lonely, Lord. Help us to shatter that loneliness with Your love.

Thanks for the Miracle

*I*t's a miracle, Lord. Yesterday she was nearly dead. Today she is alert, moving about, and soon will be going home! At seventy-seven that's quite a recovery. The miracle worker seems so simple, yet was so long in coming. A pacemaker to regulate the heartbeat is what it is called. You're behind it, Lord. You gave men minds to explore and discover and use in order to conquer illness. How thankful we are for Your gracious gift of the human mind as well as for those who use them after Your will! Again we have witnessed Your mercy, love, and revelation as the product of Your provision; and man's mind is used to give meaning to human life. Now a wise and dear friend will survive yet a while to bless us here on earth. Thank You, Lord, for the miracle You have allowed us to witness.

Prayer for Former Marrieds on Remarrying

They are to be married tonight, Father. He is a widower who has experienced the joy of a lovely home and the happiness of a child. She is a divorcee who gave her first marriage all she possibly could only to be betrayed by her chosen life's partner. She has known both happiness and bitterness in the marriage bond. He is stable, Lord. A clean cut fellow by human standards, he will make a good husband for her.

She will be good for him also, Father. There will be adjustments for each to make and habits to get used to. There will be the inevitable frictions with children. But they're mature now, Lord. Their experiences will enable them to handle wisely what they face.

Give them patience with one another, Lord. That grand ingredient is so necessary for us humans in our relationships with each other.

Give them a predominant optimism, Lord. Pessimism will always occur on occasion, causing its doubts and worries and depressions. But don't leave them with the mechanisms of pessimism to destroy them. Present them with a spirit of optimism to guide them. Give them growing appreciation for one another. They will soon make those secret discoveries which always come when intimate relationships begin. Help them to appreciate the good things they discover and to major on them so that the unpleasant things may not sow the seeds of destruction.

Inspire them to stronger faith, Lord. Deliver them from the feelings of failure which have dominated them in the past and give them the ability to trust You and life and each other.

Help them to grow together, not apart. Only thus can they establish a home that will endure and stand the tests of time.

Union Pressure

*H*e's weary, Lord. For a long time he's had to deal with tough men. Now things are tight and the union demands are rough. He's a very sensitive man. Any decision he makes from his present position will cause hardships on someone. As manager of the company, he has to act. If he does what the union demands, he will cause problems for the company. If he does what the company demands, he'll have problems with the union.

It seems an impossible position, Lord. How is a man supposed to stand such pressure? He wants to do what is right by all parties. Any way will be costly.

All I can do is ask for Your guidance for him. Give him a clear, keen mind. Grant him sure wisdom. Endow him with a noble spirit. And undergird him with the gift of peace.

The darkest hour we face, Lord, is the hour of great decision. He's at that hour now. Lead him safely through for Your glory.

The Hurting Husband

*H*e's torn apart, Lord. Like a man on the run, he flees from a bad situation. Home life has been hell for him the past twelve years. Mistakes by someone he once loved have crushed him, embittered him, emptied him, and left him a wreck.

Now it is coming to an end. He's divorcing her, Lord. I don't know how to advise him. So much wrong has transpired. There have been many years of built-up hurts and angers. Maybe parting is best.

Still, Lord, he needs to look hard at himself. He needs to find the meaning of forgiveness, the way of trust, the path to peace.

Unknowingly, he is turning his children against her. Just the little glimpses of joy that come when the children have difficulties with her are evidence of his attitude that says, "She is getting what she deserves." For those children, torn between the two, it is easy to drift to him and away from her when what they read in him is approval and happiness at their rejection of their mother.

There's so much wrong all through it, Lord. What can the

Christian faith say or do? Is there any power of reconciliation for this broken home and hurting situation?

It's gone far, Lord. The broken pieces of many lives lie scattered around like fallout from a giant explosion. Somehow, lead each person to take those broken pieces and rebuild a life more worthy of Your lordship. Only in You and with You can the sadness of this situation be turned to usefulness and gladness. Only in You can he find himself, and be made whole and strong.

Divorced Persons
and the Church

We're so cruel to each other, Lord. One human makes a mistake, steps beyond what is socially acceptable; and though that person "suffers for the sin," we will not allow full restoration. We hold the "sin" against him and make him a second-class citizen. Our cruel judgments shut folks off from You, Lord.

That's what happened to the fine couple I met today. The mistake of a too early marriage led to another, divorce. Both of them were teenagers, mere children, at that first marriage. Now they're grown up, have found themselves and each other, and have joined their lives in a second marriage union. They love each other maturely and profoundly. But Lord, their church has expelled them, cast them out. No longer are they welcome in that congregation of sinners saved by Your grace. It seems that their "sin" of remarriage after divorce is the cardinal sin.

They're miserable about it, Lord. How can they found an enduring home apart from strong support of the fellowship? How can they live lives of stability when the church refuses to forgive and restore and redeem?

Is it right for the church to pile on added guilt, guilt which can destroy their spirits and their marriage? Where, oh, where is the forgiving spirit of Jesus in such an attitude? It isn't right to divorce a life partner for just any cause. But it isn't right to cut the divorced person off from communion and fellowship, either.

Somehow, Lord, help me to help this distraught couple find themselves and You. Lead us to the light of truth and enable us to live by it no matter how hard.

Forgive the congregation that is so harsh, so like the Pharisees You had to deal with.

Somehow let us all learn the art of healing the wounds of broken hearts, broken lives, broken homes. For only therein are we like You, Lord, who gave the example of binding up the wounds of human hurts and tortured spirits and lives.

The Special Child

*H*er heart breaks, Lord. She loves the little girl but realizes that she'll never be "normal" as other children. So her mother-heart that dreams of frilly dresses and dainty little girl graces just breaks. The little eight-year-old, hundred pound girl will never be dainty and graceful. She is mentally slow, physically abnormal, clumsy, and extremely large.

Her life span is questionable. Her future health is questionable. Her ability ever to fulfill her role of womanhood is almost impossible. Yet, Lord, she's a wonder. She knows love and shares it. She cares about people. She's so open and honest about all things. She's not cumbered by a lot of hang-ups under which others labor. It's refreshing to watch this special, clumsy child as she copes with her handicaps. It renews faith in human ability.

And certainly it taps the well of human compassion and concern to watch her move bravely and joyfully through each day.

Her mother fears for her, Lord. Help the mother to trust her to You.

Her mother feels cheated, Lord. Her dream world of a physically beautiful child is still a dream. Help the mother to accept the beauty of this child's spirit and outlook. Help her to know that this kind of beauty is far more to be desired than physical beauty, which so often leads to vanity and false pride and eventual deep hurt.

It's hard for the mother, Lord. She's given love and care these eight years and will continue to do so. Her burden is heavy and will not grow any lighter with the passing of the years.

Somehow, as only You can, give her strength and love and peace to endure the task ahead. Help her to be thankful for this special child, even as we are thankful to You for giving her to us for a season.

The Human Blessing

*H*e sat there in the sunshine, Lord, fondling his cane and gazing contentedly at the distant mountains. He isn't financially rich. In fact, he is very poor by worldly standards. But in every other way, he's rich, Lord. It doesn't take long to discover that he is wealthy in faith, humility, courage, honesty, and wisdom.

His one great asset that eclipses all others is his generosity. He gives lavishly of himself though he feels he hasn't much to give.

He's a blessing to humanity, Lord. I'm glad that our paths have crossed and recrossed.

I've seen him in desperate pain but never heard him complain. I've heard him speak kindly while others raged. I've known him to comfort others just by his presence.

He's been sick a long time, Lord. But that sickness hasn't made him bitter. He hasn't lost faith, but gained it. Through his pain others have been enlightened and some even healed of their inward rebellion.

We have been blessed by him, Lord, more than we realize. Now the circle of activity is growing smaller. Soon the disease will make him totally disabled. Many folks will forget him until it is too late here on earth to express appreciation.

We're that way, Lord,—careless, procrastinating humans. But all of us who have been touched by his generous, loving spirit will recall him with fondness and will never be the same since he stepped into our lives with a smile, a word of cheer, and a spirit of genuine good will.

He's just sitting there, Lord, gazing at the distant mountains waiting for his next opportunity to lift some weary pilgrim. While he waits, lift him, Lord. Keep his spirit from being destroyed. We need his kind in our world. We need those saints who sit and wait and draw close to You, that through them we might draw close, too.

Prayer for
an Aged Mother

She's old now, Lord. Age has slowed her step, dimmed her eye, and dulled her hearing. Time was when she walked briskly, saw far, and heard clearly. That was when she felt the heavy responsibility of parenthood. Children's demands were then met with decisive action and deep trust.

The years have worn her down. Bravely did she face the massive responsibilities of rearing a large family alone. Resolutely did she prepare her children to be contributing assets to society. Diligently did she instill in them the attributes of honesty, hard work, deep faith, and acting concern.

Now the children are grown, gone and on their own, Lord. She's alone at the close of life. Just a few memories keep her company. She doesn't dwell in the shimmer of past glories. I doubt that she would see her toil through the years as having been heroic. It was her duty and she did it. Even though the future for her is not so long as the past has been, she looks outward toward tomorrow.

It is beautiful, Lord. These days for her, called the golden years, have not diminished her capacity to hope and dream and plan. She says there's still some task for her or she wouldn't be here. That's faith, Lord—inspiring faith.

While now we have to tell her what she's looking at, interpret clearly what we're talking about, and set the pace more slowly for her—may we never forget the anxieties she's felt for us, the times she's worried over us, the places she's prayed for us, the lessons she's taught to us, the faith she's given to us. She's made us in large measure what we are, Lord. And she's done her job well.

She's old, Lord. Soon the clear bell-note will sound for her and she will confidently turn to follow its peal. We'll miss her from among us; but we'll know, Lord, that her life and all her efforts were not in vain.

The Departing Soldier

*I*t was a sad moment for them, Lord. The time to leave for a
tour of military duty halfway around the world had come.
Twelve long months they will be separated.

He's a brave young man. Strength seems to flow from him
to those near. She is supported by that strength, Lord. Her
impaired vision has limited her, and he has in part been her
eyes for quite some time. Through the times of testing and
trial, it is evident that they have become quite close. But
now they must part.

Pray, Lord, give to this dedicated soldier the presence of
Your Spirit as he leaves home and family and fellow pilgrims
for a while. Keep him strong in his faith, free from falling
into temptations, true to his vows to his country, wife, child,
and God.

He'll be faced with lonely hours and enticing interludes.
He's human, Lord, very human. When the protective forces
of home, church, society are not present, it is easy to yield
to the lure of evil. Please, Lord, be his constant companion
of strong conviction, high ideals, and enduring love as he
fulfills his duty to his country in a far-off and strange land.

Let her know You are constantly with her, Lord. Loneliness will invade her life, too. The absence of someone on whom she depends will make her daily routine difficult. Raising a little boy for one year alone will tax her energies and her strength.

She needs strength and guidance from beyond herself. We will all do what we can to assist her. But, Lord, we so soon forget the needy, the lonely, the waiting souls. Be present for her in these months ahead.

If You abide in him and in her, and if they abide in You, strength, hope, love, and triumph will be their rich reward when they are together again.

The Desperate Husband

*H*e's about at his rope's end, Lord. Seven years is a long time to live in suspense, under pressure, and financially bound. His terminally ill wife doesn't want to be the burden she is to him. In her way she tries to make things as easy as possible.

But, Lord, there is no easy way for any human being to take away that desperate feeling he possesses and recognizes. He can't sleep soundly, work well, relax often, or forget for a while. He just has to live with this burden—this heavy responsibility—and it isn't easy.

I'd like to carry it for him for a while if I could. But that can't be. All I can do is listen helplessly as he pours out the anguish of his soul, takes another grip on life, and starts out again. I bring his case to You, Lord. Somehow faith has taught me that You can sustain him. Do for him what no one else can do. Give him peace and assurance that You are with him. He needs that, Lord. And use me if You need me, to be Your instrument in helping him through this hard, hard place in life.

The Return of the Children

*T*oday the children came back, Lord.
They were small and some were afraid.
Others were adventurous,
        asking questions,
        making observations,
        exploring corners.

Mothers, some with a tinge of sadness, stood about
        as if they did not know what would be expected of
        them.
You understand that, Lord.

You know, as many of us have learned, that the
        children have taken a big step.
Some have been pushed.
Some have willingly ventured forth,
        but all of them have begun a new pilgrimage.
They will not go home the same little fellows because
        now they have been to school.

Those mothers, Lord, need strength and courage today.
Some need it more than others; yet each of them will need
Your help because now her child does not belong to
her alone anymore.
The child has in a very real sense entered the world.

Give the teachers wisdom to direct their little minds wisely.
Let them see the magnitude of their trust.
And where human frailty errs, may divine strength sustain.
Thank You, Lord, for the children.
Thank You for letting us have them for this small moment
of their lives.
Give us grace to lay wisely this foundation stone on which
they will stand.

The Church

The Church frustrates me, Lord.
Somehow it seems to have lost its way.
The folks who make up its membership are so nonchalant
    about it.
Some seem shallow,
    some confused,
    some hostile,
    some dedicated.

I wonder, Lord, what makes the Church the focal point of
    men's rejection?
They come and follow gladly for a while—then they are gone.
The early luster of zeal gives way to the full presence of
    apathy.
Why, Lord?
Why can't folks be faithful?
Does the truth drive men away?
Or is it that we who lead are afraid of the truth and couch
    it in thoughts too broad for men to grasp?

I don't know, Lord, but I worry about the lack of concern
    shown for the Church, Your body.
Maybe that's it, Lord.
Maybe after nearly two millennia, men still treat You as they
    always have.
I remember how they flocked to You on Monday when You
    were meeting their needs.
And I also remember how they deserted You on Friday when
    You needed them.

No, we haven't changed much, Lord.
We're still the fickle crowd,
    the selfish crowd,
    the impatient crowd
    that cannot wait for Your will to be done through us.

Forgive us, Lord; forgive us.
So many of us do not know what we're doing to You again.
If we did, then maybe we would love the Church instead of
    ignoring it and forgetting it
      and letting so much else claim us for a moment
      when You want to claim us for eternity.

Frailties

*H*uman frailty is hard for us to take, Lord. We have been taught from our youngest years that there is something wrong in being tired, in getting sick, or in needing skilled hands to minister to us.

Too many folks see these frailties as human weakness. But Lord, some have learned that it is only when the frailties declare our limits that we learn to live by faith.

It is only when weakness calms our hurried lives to a halt that we find Your strength sufficient.

Our frailties frighten us, Lord. Our weaknesses, especially in our physical makeup, embarrass us.

Help us to overcome such human foolishness and in frailty and weaknesses find Your purpose. Then we will "be strong though weak, faithful though frail."

The Lost Dream
of Motherhood

She's just a young woman, Lord. Her dream of a family of her own runs strong. But today the dream must die. Disease demands the removal of vital reproductive organs. Her ability to conceive and give birth to a child is gone.

She asked me what she would do now.

I can give her the standard answers. I tell her that life isn't over, that her energies can be directed toward worthwhile causes, that she can use her time developing a career. But Lord, I can't tell her what to do with the broken dream.

I can't help her find any way to fulfillment of her life-long hopes of motherhood. I can't help her take away the loss she feels and that her young husband must now live with.

She thinks he will feel cheated. No children of his own will ever cheer him or delight his homecoming. That hurts her, Lord. The gift of life was what she so desperately wanted to give. Now she can't.

For her, a meaningful part of her life has been denied her. Today, the future seems dark and hopeless.

She's so young, Lord. There are years in front of her. I don't know what to tell her to do, or what to feel, or how to think. All I can tell her is to let You know how much she aches at this loss, how frightened she is, how disappointed she feels, how useless her life now seems.

Please listen to her, Lord, for she is so very young, and You alone can soothe her aching soul, calm her fretful fears, give her inward courage. Only You can help her to become the useful, lovely person she is still capable of being.

She needs You, Lord, Your love, Your direction, and above all, Your vision of possibilities.

Prayer for
the Dying Woman

She knows she's dying, Lord. No one has dared tell her.
Each seems to feel it would be cruel or shocking or emotional to talk about this ultimate in life, especially with someone who is known to be in death's grip.

But she knows, Lord. She has seen her strength fail and not
return.

She has noticed the increasing pill bottles which clutter
her bedside table. She knows she's dying, Lord. In her eyes
is that burning question. Her unnaturally high-pitched
voice disguises the raging fear she wants to let out. Her
nervous hands flay about longing for some strong hand to
hold to.

She needs assurance, Lord—Your kind of assurance. Ours
is not enough. For we are afraid, too. Her situation is a threat
to all of us. It's so final, so lasting, so all-consuming.

So, Lord, we sit and exchange banal words. We evade the
real fear, both mine and hers. Use me to open the door for
her hostilities and fears to leave by. Give me the courage to
talk to her about what is most important to her.

I'll try to be the strong hand she needs in her fearful,
desperate hour.

I'll try to be the assurer of eternal life.

I'll try to help this fellow pilgrim through this lonely place.

You lead, Lord; I'll try to follow. She's dying, Lord; she knows it. And a little bit of me is dying, too.

The Troublemaker

She's a problem, Lord. She means well I suppose, but her well-meaning intentions certainly stir up a lot of dissension. Maybe she's a calculating troublemaker. If that is her attitude, help me to be strong enough to face her, honest enough to deal with her, and loving enough to forgive her.

I know she wants to be in the limelight. That's been her desire and ambition all her days. She does have talent. Some of her talents have faded with the passing years. Maybe that is her problem. Maybe she can't bear the truth that she no longer can perform as once she did. Out of that has come jealousy toward anyone who excels where she no longer can excel.

Lord, it hurts anyone to recognize the truth about themselves. She's hurting now, and in a very real sense is suffering because she lives too much in the past. Somehow, turn her attention around and point her to the possibilities of the present. That is the only way she can ever find peace and purpose and learn to accept herself as worthwhile, and others as capable.

Fear of Failure

I'm afraid, Lord. Afraid of failure and afraid of the routine boredom with which life seems filled. Failure has always seemed like a weakness to me. I don't know why, but it has. In this endless task of dealing with people, I get frustrated and bored with the same routine over and over.

Where has the excitement gone, Lord?

Where is the thrill and joy that once sang like a morning song in my soul?

Has familiarity with the vessels I handle caused them to become tarnished? I don't know the root cause. I don't understand the foundation of doubt. I can't fathom the struggle I am in.

But You, Lord, know the inner workings of my soul. You know the deeper longings of my heart. You know the conflicts of my mind.

To You I give them all today, as best I can. Work through the ways You choose to bring me to where You would have me be.

Then will I have again a quiet heart, a joyful spirit, a singing soul. And all will be Your great gift to me.

The Boy from
the Broken Home

*H*e's a big burly fellow, Lord. There is no pretense about
him. From the outside he seems to be in control. He doesn't
complain, he doesn't brag, he doesn't threaten. To others he
appears to be just a big, plodding fellow.

No one would think, to look at this man-child, that he cares
much about anything. But he does care, Lord. Yesterday he
pulled aside the mask behind which he lives and poured out
his heart to me.

He's hurting—way down deep inside, he's hurting. Here
is a fellow caught between the angers of his parents. They
can't make it together, and this nineteen-year-old has to taste
their wrath.

Now his father has left, and today he is saddled with the
care of a semi-invalid mother.

His dream, he said, was to be a mechanic. All the plans
had been made for him to learn that trade. Now, that dream
has about blown away.

It isn't right, Lord. He is bearing the results of his parents'
sins and he doesn't know why.

I know the theological, philosophical answers. But, Lord,

I don't know the heart answers. I can't remove the problem splinters and bind up the wound and make him well.

All I can do is listen as he unloads his hurts, angers, fears, and feelings.

And I can sit down beside him and cry with him.

He needs Your strength, Lord. His isn't sufficient. His faith needs today to be vindicated.

Stand with him, Lord. Stand with him.

He's a big burly fellow.

He's strong.

But without You, he is going to fall, maybe never to rise again.

The Grieving Widow

She loved him, Lord.
Together they had many fine years.
Then last year his earthly journey ended.
Today, he has been dead one year.
That brings back all the heavy sense of loss,
    all the memories,
    all the dreams.

And it's hard for her, Lord.
She has done well, this past year.
Her attitude has challenged many,
    consoled some,
    changed others.
But today, Lord, the brave front is gone for a while.
Thank You for such experiences.
Out of them we see our humanity,
    our frailty,
    our fright.

We learn that we cannot go it alone, build up a strong resis-
    tance, construct a new life, and mold a new lifestyle by
    ourselves.

We need You on hard days like this.
She needs You—Your comfort, Your strength, Your love.
Let it shine in her life today.
She loved him, Lord.
She loves You, too.

Details

Details. They sometimes get to be a load, Lord. The tape and pins, the pencils and paper, the meeting times and re-minder letters—they stack up!

Keep me aware of their importance. Help me to remember that the details of the enterprise are the foundation stones on which we build.

They're the cement that holds the structure together.

They're the wires of communication that keep everyone informed.

But, Lord, how I'd like to cast them aside! How I like to do the "big" things that are exciting and uplifting!

Give me a new appreciation for details, Lord.

Then they, too, will become exciting, and their results will be uplifting.

Confession

Confession is hard for proud men, Lord. We do not like to look at ourselves honestly, face our faults squarely, name our sins openly.

It is easier for us to turn our heads from searching truth, ignore condemning conscience, follow nameless passions. Yet the load our sins place on us is smothering.

We cannot move as freely, walk as far, enjoy as much, or see the glory which should be ours in life.

Disturb us with Your presence until we have called them what they are.

Give us vision to see their destructive harm, wisdom to cast them aside, humility to seek forgiveness at Your hand as we learn to confess to You our sins and thus find new life through Christ, our Lord.

The New Baby

*H*e's so tiny, Lord. Why, I can hold him in one hand: Yet he's alive, alert, and on his way down the journey of life.

We will never understand the miracle of the creation of a child. It is a mystery too deep to comprehend. While we may be able to grasp the biological, psychological, emotional aspects of conception and birth, we are in the dark of mystery when it comes to understanding the reasons and sources of life. All we can do is accept it as a gift from You, Lord, and then seek to make the lives entrusted to our care meaningful, useful, and purposeful.

That is our prayer for the fine couple who was blessed this week with a new son. He's an individual, Lord. He will develop a mind and spirit unique unto himself. He will dream his own personal dreams and have his own secret hopes. Along the journey to maturity, he will experience disciplines in his personal way and will respond to them after his own fashion. As a mature adult, he will make personal decisions and personal choices that will affect the society in which he lives, as well as himself and his destiny. We are all thankful that he is an individual, unique unto himself.

Yet, even so, he must learn the art of responsibility to the society in which he lives. He must learn to love, to show concern, to care, and to help those of the broader family of man as they struggle along. And he will have to learn also, to accept their responding love and care and help. He doesn't come equipped with those attributes, Lord, only with the capacity to develop them.

Help his fine parents to have the wisdom, the courage, and insight, and the ability to instill in his developing personality the high moral and ethical values of Christ. Help them to take this complicated little organism of a baby and mold it into a fine, worthy, useful person who will be an asset to himself, to his world, and above all else, to Your kingdom.

He has a long journey ahead of him, Lord. Give all of us who touch his life the ability to touch it worthily.

Prayer for
the Country Preacher

*H*e stood there, Lord, his big mechanic's hands gripping the sides of the pulpit as if he were about to fall. In front of him on the stand lay a well-worn Bible. Its edges were tattered, its cover smudged, and its binding extremely loose. Occasionally, he would gently pick up the book before him with a tenderness and love as if he were lifting a new born baby or handling some priceless treasure.

As he spoke, it became evident that he knew what was in the book he so lovingly caressed. He doesn't have a polished education. His speech is not free from grammatical errors. His arrangement of thoughts gives evidence of a lack of skill in such matters. But, Lord, as I listened to this Christian man tell of his experiences in the faith, I heard a masterpiece of loving devotion. With homely phrases and vivid accounts, he wove the story of his pilgrimage. Occasionally, (with an embarrassed apology) he explained his knowledge of the fact that he had little formal education.

Yet he knows as we all know, that the time for learning is far gone. Age has given him responsibilities and imposed limitations which preclude any more formal training. But, Lord, I am thankful for him just as he is. He reminds me of the early disciples of the Lord. His sincere, honest explanation of what he has found in the faith is more powerful than many eloquent lectures on the subject. With his life he expresses his faith in the Lord Christ. With his lips he tries with all his power to express what fills his soul.

Use him, Lord, even as You use all who are willing to let You have direction for their lives.

He's a big, gentle, lovable man, Lord. And his simple faith, his homely expressions, his vibrant love for Christ and man are captivating indeed.

The Encounter
with Youth

*H*as it been twenty years, Lord? Why, it seems but yester-day that I sat where these fresh-faced, bright young people are sitting. Now I find myself standing before them trying to give something of guidance as they seek Your will for them.

They have come from varied religious backgrounds, Lord. There are Protestants, Catholics, Jews, and seekers among this gathering of Baptists. Somehow the differences just aren't so evident. They are all eager to know how they might walk in Your ways.

Thank You, Lord, for this fine opportunity. Thank You for the way You have led me through the years so that it would now seem that I have something to share. Thank You for these winsome children of the "next generation." They're open, inquisitive, serious, and searching while maintaining a joy at being alive. Oh, I know that beneath the veneer of sophistication there are the struggling, frightened spirits seeking some word of security and peace. But, Lord, they're learning to cope rationally with the lurking monster that is present in so many of us.

Now I ask for Your Spirit to encounter us in our search for Your will. Let the hours we spend together be filled with a glory of apprehension. Let those faltering and struggling to find You make the grand discovery of Your presence and love for them. Somehow in this place, let new hopes be born as new visions for life are gained which are in keeping with the desires of the Lord Christ.

They're young, Lord, and they have come searching. Pray that they may not be disappointed and frustrated now or down the corridor of the years as they seek to know and do Your will.

The Suddenly Grown Child

There she was, Lord, running out onto the court, immaculate in her white uniform trimmed in red, hair bundled in pig-tailed fashion, and a gleam of delight on her face. At last a long held dream had come true. She was actually playing on her school basketball team. And Lord, I'll have to admit that I saw her through a bit of a haze. I was proud of her, glad for her, so proud that a few tears clouded my vision. But the haze was deeper than the few tears I had to blink back. For I was looking back at the road along which she had come in twelve brief years to begin playing her part as a team member. And I saw again that little baby sleeping peacefully in a hospital crib a few hours after birth. I was watching again as a small infant struggled first to sit up, then to stand for the first time. Again I saw the glad look of accomplishment when at last she took her first step alone. How could I ever forget the daily "story-time" when she would bring her favorite book, crawl on my knee and demand to be read to. Again I saw the little girl trudging up the sidewalk, book satchel in hand, on her way to school. And I remember the hard tug at my heart because I knew that she was now a part of a world where others would give her the major portion of her guidance.

So it has been, Lord, that through the years I have watched this special and beloved little girl steadily climb from one achievement to another. Tonight she is extremely happy, and I am very proud of her.

Just guide her on, Lord, I pray. So much that she will seek to know and do is beyond my abilities now. All I can do is trust her, place her in Your care, and be proud of her when she reaches a goal for which she struggles.

The Unwed Mother

She's so young, Lord. She's really just a child. Yet she has all the physical attributes of a young woman. Because her body grew up before her emotions and her judgment, she has wound up in trouble. Her passions and drives got out of control, and soon she will bear a child out of wedlock. For several months we have tried to deal with the emotions of the situation. We have studied all the courses of action we could take, and she is aware of the cost of any decision she must make about the future of the child. And today she has made her decision. The child will be given up for adoption. So here we are again trying to deal with the emotions of a fifteen-year-old little girl after she has made her decision. How can she be helped through this difficult hour of parting with a child to which she was given life?

"You can help her most by simply caring about her. Words will not suffice. Presence is what is needed. She feels rejected by those she loves most because they are having a hard time dealing with the situation, too. She knows she has broken the rules. She knows the stigma this will bring, and she is suffering terribly for what she has caused. And she knows that she will have to live with this decision for the remainder

of her life. Right now she needs you to accept her as a person —not judging, not condemning, just accepting. Then she will know that there is at least one person who might begin to understand and help her to understand. I am aware that to care for one so burdened under guilt and rejection is a weighty load. Yet I also know that your bearing her burden with her is the only way for that lost soul to reach redemption and find restoration. And she's lost today. She is haunted and hurt and lost. Yet still, I love her as if she were the only one in the world to love. But I must use you to bridge the gap that has been created between her and me. It is over the bridge of your caring and acceptance of her as a fellow pilgrim in need that I can come to her in renewed fellowship. Through your love and caring and acceptance, she will experience my forgiveness. Care for her as in Christ you have found that I care for you. That is the privilege of a disciple."

I do care, Lord. And I shall go to her and sit there on the ground beside her. And I shall share her loneliness. I shall cry with her. I will love her in Your strength. Then I shall walk with her through the dark shadows of her haunting fears and condemning doubts until she emerges again into the glory of Your new day for her.

The Beggar

*H*ow can a fellow tell the difference between the legitimate down and out and the out-and-out bum, Lord? Like the fellow who came by today. He had a good story. His low-paying job barely covered family expenses, and he heard that things were better in the big city. So he left everything to try for the high-paying job. Only there was no job available. Now he is stranded and needs help to get home. He would even work for a few hours to earn a little money if he could get a job. What do we do, Lord?

"Well, son, give the man the benefit of the doubt. Check him as closely as you can and on the basis of your instinct about the situation, try to meet his need. You may be taken in by a freeloader, but you also may be giving aid to an angel unawares. And no matter if you do get taken in, is it not still more blessed for you to give than to receive? The few dollars and the meager minutes will not be lost. You can afford to share from your great over-abundance. The time is really mine, and when you use it to help some destitute soul along the way, you are doing my will. Never turn a beggar away empty handed. For love at its best is still one beggar sharing his crust of bread with another. Freely have you received, so *freely give. Then leave the ultimate outcome to me, and I promise you that the bread you cast upon the waters will come back to you again."*

I understand, Lord. Forgive me for judging—for bearing the name of servant yet seeking ways to withhold human service instead of giving it. Forgive me for the veil of distrust which falls over my spirit when strangers who beg come to me for what help I can give. Forgive me for viewing any human soul as being less than divine. Thank You, Father, for reminding me that "in as much as I do it unto the least of these, my brethren, I do it unto You."

The Dreamer

*H*ere he is, Lord, standing at the dawning of life, scanning the mysterious horizons before him with awe and anticipation. High expectations of what that onrushing horizon offers thrill him. Great hopes of what the events of life can be molded into surge through his efforts. With keen anticipation glowing on his face, he stands gazing outward at life with all its high calling, all its possibilities, all its promise. He is a dreamer, Lord. And all the pent-up energies of youth lean eagerly toward the life to come that they may be released and used and renewed.

How we rejoice in this young dreamer! Something of his expectant enthusiasm inspires us. Something of his untarnished idealism recalls our own high dreams and pure hopes. Something of his yearning to achieve gives us the courage to try again. He is a blessing, Lord, an unexpected blessing rising to grace our lives.

Our experiences with life have taught us that far too many dreams so soon fade, the grand hopes so soon vanish, and the high ideals so easily fall in the journey down this road of life we all must travel. But, Lord, enable us to somehow help this inspiring dreamer never to lose what he has. He has looked long and hard and dreamed high. He has coupled his dream to strong faith in You and believes with all his heart and soul that his high dreams can become realities.

When he becomes discouraged, give us the grace to encourage.

When he loses hope, give us the ability to rekindle his fires of hope.

When he questions high ideals, make us wise enough to point him again to the One who is the embodiment of their fulfillment.

When his vision fades, help some pilgrim of the way to clearly restore it again.

For we need great dreamers, Lord. Not just dreamers who soon forget their dreams, but dreamers who are willing to expend the effort to make high, noble dreams come true.

He's that kind, Lord. Pray keep him ever growing, ever dreaming and ever accomplishing Your high purpose through him.

He is standing clear-eyed and eager at the morning gate of life. Let him be that way also when he comes to the evening gate, Lord. Then he will not have lived in vain.

The Man
Who Is
Different

We can't understand him, Lord. He is different from us. Through he has lived among us all his life and in many ways acts like all the rest of us, he's different. He is a homosexual, Lord. How did he come to be such? What quirk of nature or life cast him in that mold? If only we knew, maybe we could help him.

For he does not like being what he is. He knows abuse and degradation and shame such as few of us will ever know. He wants to be "straight," but cannot quite make the grade. The agony of his dilemma has driven him to drugs and drink and haunting despair. Several times he has approached the brink of suicide. He doesn't like anything about this hideous drive that consumes him.

Lord, he is so talented. Sensitivity is a strong trademark of his character. Friendliness is a trait which overflows from him to those about him. He has so very much to offer and would be able to do so if he did not have this terrible basic problem which leads on to other problems and makes his life absolutely miserable.

He loves You, Lord. Yet while he loves You, he knows that this present condition is separating him from expressions of Your love in him. He knows that he is hurting You and Your church with all its people who care about him. So the guilt piles up, layer on heavy layer, until the burden is about to crush him.

All we can do, Lord, is care about him. Many of us will try to help him and accept him as he is with the hope that he can be made new. That will have to be done by Your Spirit, Lord. We'll listen and try to help all we can, but we cannot renew the spirit of a fallen man.

So our prayer is that You will begin to work in him with a power we long to see at work in its renewal efforts. We bring him to You, Lord of love. You understand what we can never begin to comprehend, and we lay him at Your throne of redemption and new life.

He is miserable, Lord. Please make him joyful as You deal with his soul and spirit, making him new.

The Crippled Boy

*H*e just wants to go fishing, Lord. But to any casual ob-
server it is obvious that long months will pass before this
brave little seven-year-old lad will hold a fishing pole in his
hand. An explosion in his home some four years ago has
crippled him for life. Limbs are crooked, burn scars are evident, and hope for full recovery of his powers of mobility is
gone.

Today he sits in a wheel chair, his head bandaged in thick
gauze, and one arm strapped to his chest so that flesh will
grow on the arm. When the proper time comes, he will have
to go through several more operations to separate that arm
from his chest. And all of that will postpone his fishing trip to
the quiet waters of his south Georgia home for a long time.

So this morning I bring him to You, this little boy of great
suffering. He has been patient with that bewildered patience
of a child who doesn't understand everything that is hap-
pening to him. He has endured suffering at this beginning of
life with more character than many show who have jour-
neyed far along the way. But, Lord, he wants to get away—
he wants to go fishing. He wants to be back in those familiar
places his boy-heart loves. He is tired of sterile rooms, glar-

ing lights, honking horns, and endless days of confinement
to a sick room. He wants to run free and feel again the warm
breeze blowing across the pond against his face. He wants
to be a boy who is whole, Lord.

It is obvious to those who see him that he will one day be
up and out and about. But right now there is no way to grant
the gift of wholeness and freedom and home which he so desires. All that can be done is to employ the wonderful mira-
cles of healing and repair that have been revealed to us. As
they have been used diligently in the past for his benefit,
may they be applied with equal diligence in the future. And
Lord, where human wisdom and skill leave off, may Your
infinite wisdom and care meet the needs which frail, short-
sighted people cannot meet. With Your help and guidance
coupled with the skill and knowledge You have revealed to
us, may he soon be healed and made able to romp and play
as a little boy should.

He just asked to be able to go fishing, Lord, but his heart
is crying out to be made whole and free again from pain and
suffering. May his heart-cry be heard and his soul-longing
soon be satisfied.

Young Love Lost

*H*e has tasted love spurned, Lord. In trust he extended his heart to one whose very presence brought joy and contentment. For a while that deep love was returned. But then, as so often happens when love is young, the attraction on her part faded, and he was left to himself. Now he grieves for what can never be possessed again. All the dreams shared, all the hopes expressed, all the plans made in sharing have crumbled to dust with one act of rejection on her part. He doesn't know where to turn now. Something very precious to him has died, and he hurts more deeply than words can ever express.

Some folks have laughed at him, Lord. They call him "silly" for getting so involved. But it is no laughing matter. It is the most serious crisis he has ever faced in his young life. While we know that he will survive and live to love another day, we also know that the memory of this first romance will never completely fade from his treasure-house of cherished memories. Another may one day claim his attention and even his heart, but always there will be that one small chamber of his mind reserved as sacred ground on which none other will be allowed to tread. In a very real way, this first, deep love will affect much that he does with the remainder of his life.

Through anger brought on by the rejection of this lost love, he can wage destructive war with life and its many calls to accomplishments; or through understanding he can grow in usefulness and accomplishment in society.

So help those of us who care about his present welfare to enable him to understand this circumstance. But as we try to help him, keep us from making light of this young love with all its idealisms, purity, and promise. For he loved her, Lord. And though it could not last for a lifetime as they grew up into mature adulthood, this first love will forever be sacred to him. Let us all see it as a wonderful, sacred gift to the young through which they grow to maturity.

And Lord, thank You for letting us remember our own bitter-sweet memories of first love.

The Fourth Decade

*I*t's a new decade for me, Lord. Somehow I would like to avoid entering it, but then time will not allow any sort of detour or delay. Here at the beginning, I am aware that this one will be different from the other three. I know that I will be more reflective, more cautious, more controlled than I have been in the past. But I also know that life will bring its rewards. Facing events with more maturity, I will not be so easily frustrated. Having seen much of both the good and the bad, I will be more able than ever to cope with events. Then too, the burning ambitions of previous years have ceased to blaze so demandingly. Position and power and wealth are not as important now as they were ten years ago. Plaudits of men and public recognition are no longer goals for which I strive. For I have found these to be passing trophies—so fleeting that today's trophy is tarnished and forgotten with tomorrow's sunrise. I know that the years of this decade can be years of peace of heart and spirit. They can be years of accomplishment free from the frustrations of needing to climb the ladder of success. They can be the most worthwhile years of my life as I try to serve You and mankind.

Yet I am aware that without the strength of Your Spirit

there can be nothing worthwhile done through me. I am aware that I must make a constant commitment to You and let You direct my paths. So here at the beginning of the fourth decade of my life, I once again give what I am and what I have to You, Lord. It isn't much, for mentally I am not so quick as I need to be, my understanding is extremely limited, and my acquired knowledge is so meager. But I am willing to have the little which You have entrusted to me used as You desire. Asking not for evidence of its effect, asking not for expressions of thanks, I simply give You what I am for Your use.

It's new decade for me, Lord. Make me able to meet the new challenges with renewed faith.

Concern

Sitting there with tears coursing down his ancient face, he was the picture of brokenhearted concern, Lord. He identified with what the speaker was saying about the great need to give Christian faith and direction to the young of the land. For he knew something of that need and carried in his compassionate heart a burden of desire to meet the need.

Perhaps he was reminded of a young son standing on the threshold of life, eagerly reaching forth to embrace all opportunities, who had suddenly been required to lay down his life on a distant battlefield.

Or perhaps he was recalling the years of love and guidance and sharing which he had given his beloved child. Maybe he was remembering again all that had been done and was now trying to discover what had been left undone as he thought of his child gone wrong.

Perhaps his heart broke because he had tasted the bitter wine of disapproval as one he loved more than he loved himself spurned all his direction and love and concern.

Perhaps in the silence of his remembering heart, he was reaching out again to embrace the darling of his life, know-

ing that open expression of his yearning soul would be re-
pulsed.

There was no way to know what tender thought, laced
with hurt and sadness, was touched. But something tripped
the key to the control of his emotions and expressed itself in
his shed tears.

And seeing the gentleness, the wisdom, and the love
etched on that ancient face, my heart, too, was deeply
touched. I wanted to reach out and lay my hand on his gently
stooped shoulders in a caring gesture. I wanted to give him
something to reassure him. But, Lord, his was a sacred
memory, too sacred to be handled by unfamiliar hands which
might permanently damage a priceless treasure. If that be
cowardice, I plead quilty. If it be succumbing to evil temptation, I am guilty. If it be procrastination, I am grossly guilty.
But if it be wisdom, I thank You for enough wisdom to remain apart and intercede with You on his behalf. For he was
deeply moved in that period of worship, Lord, and through
his tears I was brought close to him and to You in a mem-
orable, sacred moment.

The Caller

She calls often, Lord, just needing to have someone to talk to and on whom to vent her feelings and frustrations. I used to think that she was imagining much of her trouble. Then I went to her home and saw her plight. Lord, she hasn't told the half of it! She must be nearly a saint to live out the vows she made so many years ago. Sickness ravages her body, rebellion of children brings heartache, and an alcoholic husband with heart disease keeps enough tension going to do a hundred families. Yet in the midst of it all, she clings to her faith in You. She remembers those happier days when love was strong and health was good and her family practiced devotion to God. She has known what superlative living in a spiritual sense means, and that memory becomes her resting place amid the tumult of her present existence. Because she loves You, Lord, and because of what once was a reality in life, she clings to the hope that one day sanity will return to her home.

No one knows why things went wrong. Her husband blames it on the economic pressures of the times and the drain of her incurable illness. The children blame their plight and attitude on their father's drinking and accompanying meanness when intoxicated, as well as on their mother's inability to function so as to fulfill their expectations of her motherhood. A great deal of the trouble stems from ignorance and a lack of genuine commitment on their part to the high, hard, values of faith in You.

Yet no matter the reason, Lord, here in this desperate setting resides one of Your saints. Our human wish is to have the circumstances changed and the problems removed. But, Lord, we know that our ways are not Your ways, our thoughts are not Your thoughts, our desires are not Your desires. So as intelligently as we know how, we pray that You will strengthen the resolve of this lady. Increase her faith and empower her hope that she may live with some sanity even amid this turmoil. And, Lord, open the way for Your Spirit to redeem all involved in this pitiful situation. Let the miracle of change occur as You come to abide in the home of this burdened saint who calls so often, needing more help than human hands and hearts and wisdom can ever supply.

Surrender

*H*e has made peace with himself now, Lord. Facing the
possibility of a long period as an invalid with increasing
weakness overcoming him, this once robust and vigorous
man has accepted what seems to lie ahead. It wasn't easy. He
cried and complained. He cursed and blamed. He doubted
and feared. Then came that hour of total surrender—that
hour when he accepted the fact that all his rebellion and
ranting would not change the situation. He said it was the
greatest hour of his life, Lord. In that hour he, who had been
a Christian believer for so long, came to the point where trust
was fully born. He told of how he had laid his case in Your
hands, not asking for an easier road to walk, not asking for
healing in his diseased body, but simply asking, and truly
meaning, that You take him as he is and use him. There was
a deep note of joy in his voice when he told of this surrender
in all circumstances to trust. He meant it when he voiced the
agony of his Gethsemane. For the issue of life had there been
settled, and he knew that nothing more could happen to
destroy what he had found. And he means it when he says
that all he wants is for You to be glorified. If it means his
death, that is fine. If it means that he must suffer, he will bear

it gladly. He wants only to be used to reach others, however You can use him.

How inspiring those few minutes were, Lord. Having gone to minster to a friend, I left having been ministered unto. With my gigantic questions about Your justice and love, I entered the sick room where he lay. I came away reassured anew of Your love and care. Wanting to do something with my human hands to help, I was helped by divine hands extended through another's human experience.

Sharing in that moment tugged at my heartstrings. For I could not forget the anguish of a lovely wife, who tried to be brave but could not restrain her grief. I could not forget the little children with bewilderment written on their shining faces. And again I wanted to voice a protest against the meanness of circumstances that hurt innocence so deeply. But again this victorious sufferer, as if reading my innermost thoughts, offered a gentle, understanding rebuke. He said that he wanted to live, to see his children grown, but then he reminded me of how I had grown up without a father's presence. He made me aware that God who gives life cares for that life, guides that life, and sustains it. And he knows that he has already done all he can as a father to set the feet of his children on the high road of solid faith. They know where to go for help, and even though he may live, all he will be able to do is remind them of what they already know.

This was no pat answer, no gesture at rationalizing, Lord. It was the humble, contrite confession of a faithful follower of Christ who has learned to trust fully.

On his behalf, I intercede with joy and thanksgiving. I ask not that he be allowed to live, but rather that he be continually reassured of eternal life. I ask not that his circumstances be changed, but that they be useful. I ask not that the many questions asked by all be answered, but rather that the lack of answers be accepted.

I am today a little more faithful, a little more sure, and a great deal more blessed, Lord. And he is, too, because in life's desperate moment he had that hour of surrender to trust.

The Freeloader

They're perplexed, Lord. Both of them are fine Christian ladies intent on doing good works. And they have set some high examples for others to follow. But now one recipient of their care and love has become a burden by demanding more than they can give. This person imposes on their hospitality, wrecks their budgets with her demands, and destroys the sacred hours of family fellowship. I'm sure she doesn't mean to do so, Lord, but because she is lonely and somewhat ill, she feels that she has a right to make these demands. And she has become a past master at making others feel guilty when they do not respond as she demands.

Now these two good ladies are aware that they are not helping this demanding sponger to become what she should be in Your world and kingdom. They see that they are only perpetuating her present actions and making them seem to be all right. They know that she is destroying their lives with growing frustrations and driving wedges between members of their families, causing unnecessary friction.

Today, they have resolved to confront her. They love her, Lord, and this will not be easy. There will be ruptured relationships over this for a while. The one they are seeking to help will be deeply angered and hurt. So these two fine ladies need Your Spirit and guidance through this ordeal.

Give them courage to act rightly for all concerned.

Give them compassion which never forgets the primary needs of their friend.

Give them faith, knowing that you care about this situation more than any human being can ever care.

Give them love—love like unto Your own, which will be felt and seen through the entire ordeal of confrontation.

And when, led by Your Spirit, they have done what they know to be right for all parties concerned, give them peace and joy and acceptance of the wonder of the miracle of Your grace in this situation.

The Weeping Mother

She's weeping, Lord. For a long time now she has wept openly and silently. Ever since her little boy was killed in an accident, she was been inconsolable. Today she took a long hard look at the situation. Through tears expressing the mingled emotions of sorrow, fear, anger, and doubt, she cried out her agony. Wanting to blame someone and not wanting to share the responsibility of the blame, she has been hiding under the idea that this child's death was Your will. That seems to be the way her friends view it. It is even the way her very narrow and rigid view of religion explains it. In the wake of such a cruel concept of You, she has come to blame You for the agonizing hurt she feels. Close on the heels of that blame comes a suppressed anger. She cannot express that anger because she fears a worse fate for herself if she voices her feelings. She thinks it wrong to tell You how things really are with her. And, Lord, all these emotions boiling in her are about to destroy her.

Today she needs to see clearly that You are a God of infinite love. She needs to let You be a father and to understand that You are not a fiend. She needs so desperately to understand that Your perfect will never brings hurt to innocent and faithful followers. Somehow, Lord, she must discover that You have given us the freedom of decision, and because we are still slow to learn and imperfect and live in a world yet in the making, our choices sometimes bring hurt and death and destruction. This happens even when we do not intend it in any way. But she must come to understand that You will not override our choices—that You could not and still remain a father of the highest order.

O Father, some who have walked the pathway a little farther than our weeping friend, know that Your heart is sorely wounded by our hurts and distresses. Some have learned that You do not want deep hurts to come to Your children. Some have discovered, through their own trials and tribulations, that even our deepest hurts and most devastating experiences are not going to ultimately defeat us when we relinquish them to You. For in Your infinite care, You take even the most harsh experiences and weave them into the fabric of Your will for us in such a way that they become treasured assets rather than destructive liabilities. And we have discovered Your infinite love; we have grown to understanding maturity through the harsh and hurting experiences of life.

Let her make that grand discovery now, Lord. Words of direction and encouragement have been passed on to her. Thoughts concerning Your tender mercies and care have been shared with her from the wellspring of experience. Now we wait to behold the miracle of the healing of a wounded spirit as You gently and with marvelous love lead her from the jungle of dark hurt and misunderstanding to the glory of acceptance and deepened faith.

O God who weeps with those who weep, work Your miracle of Grace in her brokenhearted life that she may know also that You rejoice with those who rejoice.

The Alcoholic

*H*e came in from the street, Lord, looking for help. A few brief moments with him were enough to convince the most skeptic listener that he meant business. Alcohol has about ruined him. At thirty-two years of age, he has spent over four years in prison for alcohol related crimes. His wife has left him. Jobs are harder to keep and come less frequently. Now he becomes violent when he drinks, and unless something is done for him, he will soon be a frightening menace to society.

He sees this, Lord. He knows that because of his practice of this evil habit, his mother is a wreck, his family has rejected him, and his tomorrow is overly hopeless. So he has come to the church seeking assistance. Like a drowning man, he is crying out for a life preserver.

I am thankful that he has come. I'm glad that the church is here and gives promise of help to those in need. I'm glad and thankful that men will still see the Lord Christ as their hope. And above all, I'm thankful for the many resources we have, upon which we can rely to assist these spiritually, emotionally, physically, needy folks.

He heard about the love of the Lord Christ for him tonight. I tried, as best I know how, to plant a seed that faith and trust may be born and nourished. I pray that it may be understood. I pray that he may respond.

He's such a wreck; but Lord, You can do so much with wrecked lives. Restructure him and set him whole upon the road of life.

We'll do all we know how to help him. May he be encouraged to do his best to help himself. And where our strengths and wisdoms fail, let strength and wisdom and courage beyond ourselves be imparted to us.

He's searching, Lord. Grant him light to walk by, courage to try through, faith to believe in, and hope to cling to. Then, with Your presence he will have what is needed to live like a man again.

Morning Possibilities

*I*t's morning again, Lord. How I love the possibilities of the day! Shrouded in mystery, the unknown hours will unfold in their season and bring forth challenge and temptation, need and plenty, sorrow and joy, love and bitterness, hope and defeat, triumph and failure. There will be moments for me to serve and moments to be served. There will be periods to ponder deep thoughts and periods to act on acquired knowledge. There will be times of swift growth and times of hard, slow growth. Yet when this day is folded into the tablets of time, it will leave each of us a little older and wiser, even though we may use it foolishly and carelessly.

So this morning, Lord, I pray for a sense of sacredness about the day akin to that which You possessed as You walked among men.

I pray for keen vision of eye and mind that I may see clearly and well the task of importance that I must accomplish.

I pray that the Spirit of Wisdom will endow me with His presence that I may know how to handle each mood and situation encountered.

I pray that adequate patience will be imparted to me that I may be able to wait upon your leadership in all matters.

I pray for courage that I may be strengthened to withstand the temptations that assault me so strongly.

I pray for Your love that it may be given through me to others.

Should I, along the journey of the ensuing hours, become a victim to human weakness, Lord, give me the desire to overcome the weakness and right any wrong it may cause.

Should I fall into temptation's grasp and sin against You, let me be sensible enough to seek Your forgiveness that I may know Your restoration.

Should I today overlook some purpose and opportunity You send my way, Lord, chasten me in Your love that I may be more aware of Your presence in all things of life and thus respond more readily.

It is a new day, Lord, and I give myself to You as I begin the glory of passing through the "Hall of the Hours" that comes from You as a gift of love to be lavishly consumed.

Advent

Your coming to us is a marvel, Lord. Yet how often we miss Your entry into our lives! Turning our thoughts and faith to lesser powers, we seek glory in their passing presence. We gaze with awe at the coming of the night that man has molded with his transient hands and ignore that eternal night fashioned by hands that never fail. We view the momentary grandeur of our plastic world and overlook the eternal grandeur of Your abiding love.

Teach us, Lord, the glory of an eternal insight over a passing thought, the power of a selfless act of love over the threat of armaments massed in anger and fear, the wonder of powerful simplicities in all things over the destructive force of opulence in everything. Show us the majesty of commitment over the disaster of drifting, the sacredness of life over the curse of destruction, the meaning of giving over the treachery of getting.

Share with us anew the gift of redemption, the fact of forgiveness, the presence of Christ. Then, Lord, we lowly shepherds of the twentieth century can again marvel at that which we have seen and heard.

Christmas

*I*t's the day before Christmas, Lord, and in the village there is an air of excitement. Folks hurry from one assignment to another, making ready for the festivities that surround the celebration of the Lord's birth. Yet, amid all the excitement and wonder there are those for whom this season holds no glow of delight. Poverty has caught up with them, and their needs will not be easily met this year. Others have suffered great loss, and because of their sorrow, no joy at this Christmas pervades their lives. Still others have never caught sight of what Christmas means to the lonely heart, the broken heart, the troubled heart.

I pray, Lord, that Your matchless Spirit will guide those in need and all their kindred that something of the Christmas Spirit may come to them and transform their lives.

The Year's End

*I*t's over, Lord. The year is gone and can never be recalled
so that we can live it again. Across its days and months we
have written the story of life—according to us. Contained
within the folds of the year are stories of accomplishment and
defeat, joy and sorrow, faith and doubt, love and hate, help
and hindrance, and all the emotions of human experience.
We have known honor and debasement, felt challenge and
dullness, tasted the heady wine of purpose and the acrid salt
of disappointment.

There are days we would like to recall and multiply because of their endearment, but there are other days we would
yearn to delete because of their shame and disappointment.
Yet, Lord, all are Yours now. All we can do is remove our
hands from this spent gift of time and trust You to see,
through all that has transpired, our noble efforts and high
intentions. While we must live with our sins and failures,
please enable us to prevent them from marring our tomorrows. While we bask in the afterglow of our successes, please,
dear Lord, enable us to put them behind us that we may go
on to more noble heights of goodness and purpose in Your
world.

Make us as little children once again. Give us a fresh anticipation for the work which so soon will be upon us with the advent of the new year. Grant us a keen sense of right and wrong and strengthen us to do the right and shun the wrong. Instill in us a love of truth and an abhorrence of falsehood. Undergird us, we pray, with great and noble courage to stand for worthy and just causes even as You deliver us from cowardice, which so easily gives in to the pressures of injustice and blatant evil. Occupy us with selfless love in Christlike fashion that we may overcome hate and build stronger the kingdom of God among men.

As we turn our faces outward toward the unknown tomorrows of a new year, we join the ancient seer imploring, "Send out Your light and Your truth; let them lead me, and let them bring me to Thy holy hill" (Ps. 43:3). Following that light and knowing that truth will indeed call forth from Your children a chorus of praise for Your forgiveness, guidance, and love. Thus the new year will be made wisely useful and greatly redemptive by Your power.

A Wedding Prayer

*H*ear this day, O Lord, the eternal expressions of love as they are uttered by these Your children. As their lives are intertwined in this holy estate, we ask that Your divine love will undergird them in all their endeavors as husband and wife. Through laughter of joy and tears of sorrow, may they see Your face and feel Your arms of strength encircling them as a shield from any harm that may come to this union.

Help them to grow together. From these two who stand before us this day, may the true unity of oneness emerge. Teach them to love deeply and profoundly. When the glitter of newness and the warmth of the romantic have faded into the afterglow and living together becomes commonplace, may the fountain of understanding love and the deep channels of devotion flow into their lives to strengthen and sustain them.

Help them never to lose the sense of adventure in this thrilling journey of togetherness. As they probe its mysteries, may they experience the delight which comes from new discovery as they walk together with You on this road of life.

Let not beauty fade from their vision. Through the years may they ever see this union in the beauty of holiness, the loveliness of purity, and the grandeur of devotion. In the soft light of Your love may they ever walk the pathways of fidelity and peace.

Grant them a sense of duty. Together may they find Your destiny for them and through faith seek to fulfill Your task for them in this life. May goals be clear and their determination sure as they undertake their sacred trust for You.

Truly, may the ways of their lives and meditations of their hearts always be acceptable unto You, O Lord, our Strength and our Redeemer.